Daily Dose

DAVADE THOMPSON
&
CAMILLA DWYER

ISBN 978-1-64114-059-1 (paperback)
ISBN 978-1-64114-060-7 (digital)

Copyright © 2018 by Davade Thompson and Camilla Dwyer

All rights reserved. No part of this publication may be reproduced, distributed, or transmitted in any form or by any means, including photocopying, recording, or other electronic or mechanical methods without the prior written permission of the publisher. For permission requests, solicit the publisher via the address below.

Christian Faith Publishing, Inc.
832 Park Avenue
Meadville, PA 16335
www.christianfaithpublishing.com

Printed in the United States of America

Acknowledgments

It is with great pleasure that we take the time to acknowledge the men and women responsible for this work of art. The people whose words and actions have transformed the lives of thousands. We would like to take the opportunity to thank God first for allowing us the ability to create a piece that will impact the lives of many near and far. We would like to acknowledge our pastors and leaders, Dr. Sidrell Williams, and Joseph Ledgister for the opportunity to get to know Christ from a standpoint that was never taught or even introduced to us at any point before in our faith. Second, we would like to thank our ministers, Davade Thompson, Tuxricko Lindsay, Christpopher Edwards, Paula James, and Annette Hall for not only leading a life of exampleship but also supporting our leaders and being a support system in the body. We would also like to acknowledge brother Tajay Williams, and brother CJ Williams for allowing us to share some of their knowledge with the world.

It is with great honor that we are able to present to you the words of those that changed our lives and our mere existence. We are delighted that you will have the opportunity to experience what we did through these messages. We would also like to thank you, our audience, for your continued support and well wishes throughout our journey—we are truly grateful. Last, a special thanks goes to the members of The Holy Remnant Apostolic Church because this would not have been possible without you.

Introduction

Rudyard Kipling once said "words are, of course, the most powerful drug used by mankind." This book will introduce you to a group of people whose words have been not just a drug but an antidote. The subtle difference between a drug and an antidote is that a drug is merely a medicine or substance which has a physiological effect when ingested or otherwise introduced into the body, whereas an antidote is a remedy used for counteracting the effects of a particular poison. Though a drug is used to cure, it does not have the effect of an antidote because an antidote must be able to not only endure and fight an opposing poison but also must win to be considered successful.

The men and women responsible for writing these words are regular people just like you and me. They have changed the lives of thousands through words of encouragement by sharing the supernatural experience that they have had through Jesus Christ, which lead to the transformation of their lives, and they are eager to share it with the world in aims of changing the lives of others also. The aim of this book is to encourage, strengthen, motivate, and bring to a new dimension the understanding of life and Jesus Christ. It will help you to navigate how, through understanding Jesus' character, one will have the opportunity to build a genuine relationship with him through their own personal encounter.

These words are not of people who you see on television or on the photoshopped image on the cover of a magazine. These words are from people who have, in the most humble way possible, impacted the lives of many individuals not just with their words but through their lifestyle. I am beyond grateful to have had the opportunity to meet these individuals and even more grateful to be able to have a relationship with them. I challenge you to let these words of encouragement become a lifestyle and not just vain words that you have read. Be encouraged, be transformed, and prepare your mind to be rehabilitated with just one dose.

"Anything that requires faith is incomplete."
—Tuxricko Lindsay

"If God is blessing your neighbor, then it means he is in your neighborhood."
—Christopher Edwards

"God reveals to redeem."
—Sidrell Williams

"The tallest tree that you will find on the mountain top is the one that oftentimes goes deepest in the valley."
—Davade Thompson

"It is more dangerous to have an unknown future than a tragic past."
—Davade Thompson

"Forgiveness doesn't take away the pain, but it starts the healing process."
—Davade Thompson

"You have to fight like David in order to kill your Goliath."
—Annette Hall

"Showers of rain may not sink a ship but a single hole in the bottom will take it down."
—Davade Thompson

"Before the damage, there is a tear; before the tear, there is a pull. Don't let people pull you down, tear you apart, and damage your soul."
—Christopher Edwards

"Your miracle lies in your belief."
—Paula James

"What man sees as insignificant, God sees as an instrument for his ministry."
—Paula James

"One's capacity is never seen but revealed."
—Paula James

"Words are made to be spoken, and the mouth was made to speak. Never allow negative words to structure your future."
—Paula James

"The prerequisite for greatness is criticism and struggles."
—Paula James

"Success is locked in a room, and, in order to get to it, you have to go through the door of risk by using the key of courage."
—Tuxricko Lindsay

"Until you change your mentality, you will never change your reality."
—Davade Thompson

"When doors are open, be careful who you walk through them with."
—Davade Thompson

"Procrastination paints a portrait of failure, but commitment colors success."
—Sidrell Williams

"When vision is planted into the soil of faith and watered with consistency, it brings forth the fruit of success."
—Tuxricko Lindsay

"What's important is not what a man is, but what he is waiting to become."
—Joseph Ledgister

"My today is just a stepping stone for my divine destination."
—Paula James

"Opposition is a litmus test for success."
—Sidrell Williams

"Failure is an acquaintance that reveals true friends."
—Joseph Ledgister

"In life, all you have is each other. So, I say take care of all we have, and by that I mean take care of each other."
—Joseph Ledgister

"A beautiful face lasts for years, but a beautiful soul lasts forever."
—Joseph Ledgister

"Money doesn't make you happy, but if you don't have it, it will make you sad."
—Davade Thompson

"Every day you spend living in the past is a day you haven't lived."
—Christopher Edwards

"Don't let your flesh get a head start while your soul is still at the starting line."
—Tajay Williams

"To receive from God depends on your ability to believe in God."
—Christopher Edwards

"Great expectations require great praises."
—Christopher Edwards

"To know God is one thing, but to experience God is another."
—Christopher Edwards

"The beautiful thing with people who have walked out of your life is: while they will search the universe in vain looking for your replacement, the truth still remains. They will never find another you."
—Joseph Ledgister

"You may use someone like your crutch for a season and then throw them away, but as long as there are people with broken legs, a crutch will always have purpose."
—Joseph Ledgister

"Never allow the people who mean so little to control so much of your mind, feelings, and emotions."
—Joseph Ledgister

"If you live life putting your best foot forward, one day you'll have to make a step and your best foot will go backwards and then people will find out who you really are. Be real, be authentic, be yourself!"
—Joseph Ledgister

"Never examine your life based on people's negative remarks about you, but use it to determine the capacity of their minds."
—Paula James

"Never allow what people do or say about you change you from what you are created to be."
—Paula James

"Never settle, there is always something greater to be accomplished."
—Paula James

"Greatness is inaccessible without taking risks."
—Tuxricko Lindsay

"Never be ashamed when things seem to be falling apart, God works best with the broken."
—Paula James

"If you don't have a passion for something, then you will never know your purpose. For it is through your passion that your purpose is realized."
—Christopher Edwards

"We will never reach our true potential if we are not in harmony with passion and process."
—Paula James

"Prayer perfects your desire."
—Sidrell Williams

"When you look through the eyes of ignorance; your vision is equivalent to that of an intoxicated man."
—Joseph Ledgister

"He who hates without a cause will kill without a reason!"
—Joseph Ledgister

"Contamination of one's mind does not begin with what one hears, but the desire of wanting to hear the negative."
—Sidrell Williams

"You don't become who you are because of circumstances. You become who you are based on decisions made in your circumstances."
—Paula James

"Fear will cause you to be delayed, but faith will get you there ahead of time."
—Davade Thompson

"Be courageous and aim high. Challenges are made to strengthen you."
—Paula James

"When life hits you with struggles, fight back with prayer."
—CJ Williams

"A moment of anger can destroy years of labor."
—Davade Thompson

"Never let anger be your deciding factor. You will live to regret it."
—Paula James

"Dignity stretches the boundaries of pride."
—Sidrell Williams

"We all have two choices in life: we can either believe the truth that God says about the devil or we can believe the lies the devil says about God."
—Joseph Ledgister

"In life, we often pay the price that we pay because we dare to buy things that we cannot afford."
—Joseph Ledgister

"A man with his mind on the past cannot properly enjoy the present; consequently, he is forced to prematurely carry the burden of a future that is wrapped in uncertainty."
—Joseph Ledgister

"Impossibility is just a matter of removing God from the equation of our lives."
—Joseph Ledgister

"I've heard that opposites attract, but I say that opposites distract when purpose is not aligned."
—Joseph Ledgister

"Loyalty is a load that's not meant for everyone to bear because it rests on the strength of a person's character."
—Joseph Ledgister

"You cannot place trust in people you have a hard time figuring out."
—Tuxricko Lindsay

"Motivation and ambition is the fuel to accomplish any task."
—Paula James

"Failures are not always easy, but they make great opportunities for new beginnings."
—Paula James

"We become what consumes our mind because head knowledge is of no value if our hearts are not accepting of it."
—Paula James

"To really know someone, study their behavior and
attitude for it exposes their mind's predisposition."
—Paula James

"Some people will only pity you while you are in a pit."
—Sidrell Williams

"Opposition is nothing more than a position being opposed."
—Sidrell Williams

"Blessings begin where struggles end."
—Sidrell Williams

"In order for you to become someone else,
you must first sacrifice who you are."
—Davade Thompson

"There is nothing wrong with being in the valley as long as your eyes are still on God."
—Paula James

"A life without direction is disaster waiting to happen."
—Paula James

"Impatience always bargain for less than its worth, and
patience always reveals the true value of things."
—Tuxricko Lindsay

"Mercy ignores the cry for judgement
and echoes the need for grace."
—Joseph Ledgister

"I've realized in life that you have
Friends for the money
Friends for the fame
Friends for the bling and
Friends for the name.
Sadly, one day, you will realize
Of all the friends that came,
You don't really have a friend until
You have a friend that is still a friend in your greatest shame!"
—Joseph Ledgister

"If Jesus is for later, then Satan is for now,
and hell can be at any moment."
—Joseph Ledgister

"True loyalty is about what we endure together. It's not about who's willing to go to heaven with you; it's about those who are willing to go through hell for you."
—Joseph Ledgister

"It's not about men's favorite, but it is about who the favor of God is with."
—Davade Thompson

"An enrage from hell begins when the colorfulness of your destiny has been identified."
—Sidrell Williams

"If there is no purpose, there is no prison."
—Sidrell Williams

"If you waste time with the offenders, you will lose the gravity and integrity to color your destiny."
—Sidrell Williams

"If you fix your eyes on your pain, it closes your eyes to your destiny."
—Sidrell Williams

"No gift will ever come to perfection until you are perfected in love."
—Sidrell Williams

"Until your love is perfect in Christ, your gift will be dormant."
—Sidrell Williams

"The power of the gift is not having the gift but the execution of the gift." Sidrell Williams

"It's better to take action than to make prediction."
—Davade Thompson

"When I am in a battle, the intensity of the battle tells me that I am victorious."
—Sidrell Williams

"The goodness of God reveals the wickedness of man."
—Joseph Ledgister

"Weakness is exchanged only for strength in Christ."
—Sidrell Williams

"Unless you walk in the promise, God's shield is not activated."
—Joseph Ledgister

"Success leads to isolation."
—Joseph Ledgister

"Sometimes, the demon you are facing was not birthed by you."
—Sidrell Williams

"In the spiritual realm, an opposition is a test for success."
—Sidrell Williams

"Wherever there is an inheritance, there must be an opposition."
—Sidrell Williams

"The spirit of God will always empower you to persevere."
—Sidrell Williams

"Don't follow the trend, raise the standard."
—Davade Thompson

"If we make love a choice, we make hate an option without knowing it."
—Joseph Ledgister

"YouTube is a university."
—Davade Thompson

"Being at peace with yourself is more victorious than defeating a thousand enemies."
—Davade Thompson

"We must make love our mission in order put hatred under submission."
—Joseph Ledgister

"Love is perfect, pure, pleasant, peaceful but sometimes painful."
—Davade Thompson

"If you keep talking yourself out of everything, then you do not need an enemy to be defeated."
—Davade Thompson

"God has a way of putting this world to shame by bringing rejected people to fame."
—Davade Thompson

"Treat every opponent as an opposition to your destiny."
—Davade Thompson

"Unity is weakness to selfish people."
—Davade Thompson

"You do not need to change your feature to change your future."
—Davade Thompson

"An excuse is never the real reason for being a failure."
—Davade Thompson

"Sometimes, you don't know how good you are
at something until you start doing it."
—Davade Thompson

"As a child of God, your desire should be to
give reverence, not to get revenue."
—Davade Thompson

"Passion is the engine behind purpose."
—Davade Thompson

"Never laugh at the small size of your opponent for
they might represent something much bigger."
—Davade Thompson

"You are not rejected. You are just reserved."
—Joseph Ledgister

"The impossible is reserved for the glory of God."
—Davade Thompson

"There are two important aspects of life: one is the beginning and the other is the end. God is both."
—Davade Thompson

"Where there is a Godly inheritance there will always be giants."
—Davade Thompson

"Sometimes, silence is the best response to some questions."
—Davade Thompson

"Loneliness isn't the absence of people, but
it is having no one to help you."
—Davade Thompson

"Experience often times shuts down revelation."
—Davade Thompson

"If you keep knocking on a door and no one responds,
move on because it might be an empty room."
—Davade Thompson

"As a body, we are not in a competition but on a mission."
—Davade Thompson

"Surrendering to God is not a sign of weakness but a sign of wisdom."
—Davade Thompson

"If you obey God he will cause you to have
favor where you use to have failure."
—Davade Thompson

"What's important is not nationality but destiny."
—Davade Thompson

"Judgement without mercy for the guilty is a condemnation."
—Davade Thompson

"The more faithfully you work, the more doors will open."
—Davade Thompson

"Fire cannot burn without heat and so is destiny without desire."
—Davade Thompson

"Israel send out twelve spies, ten saw the land but believed it belongs to the giants, two saw the giants but believed the land belongs to them."
—Davade Thompson

"The friend of change is adaptability, not conformity."
—Davade Thompson

"The truth about all lies is that they will never be true."
—Davade Thompson

"Never allow your heart to lead you if your desire is wrong."
—Davade Thompson

"The perfect opportunity is one that will never come, yet it is one that you don't need."
—Davade Thompson

"No one is perfect, but unjust people think they are."
—Davade Thompson

"Many people want to be a superstar while it is still day."
—Davade Thompson

"The enemy you hide will soon expose your secret."
—Davade Thompson

"Once can be overlooked, twice deserve your attention, and thrice need to be addressed."
—Davade Thompson

"Long-term deception gives birth to sudden destruction."
—Joseph X. Ledgister

"The greatest irony in life is not that we are blind to what we are, it is the fact that even though we see, we still choose to remain blind."
—Joseph X. Ledgister

Don't be mental and choose money over potential."
—Joseph X. Ledgister

"Passion leads to prison, while purpose leads to promise."
—Joseph X. Ledgister

"Wherever you find a seed of lie that claims to bear fruits of truth, then the root has got to be deception."
—Joseph X. Ledgister

"Selfish gain can cause massive pain."
—Joseph X. Ledgister

"If God starts the fire, then he will fuel it higher."
—Joseph X. Ledgister

"Waiting on God is gonna take everything in you, but not waiting on God will take everything from you."
—Joseph X. Ledgister

"To the wrong person you will never be right, and to the right person you will never be wrong."
—Joseph X. Ledgister

"If the table refuses to turn, move your chair."
—Davade Thompson

"A living dog is better than a dead lion."
—King Solomon

"The limitations of the flesh doesn't hinder faith, but the limits of the spirit does."
—Davade Thompson

"We are oftentimes discouraged because of our unmet expectations because we overlooked the fact that many times we have exceeded our potential."
—Davade Thompson

"People often times change like night and day; they turn on and off without a switch."
—Davade Thompson

"The only way to be victorious is to walk with a purpose."
—Davade Thompson

"Contention in a leadership body is like a volcano; it starts out in the top as contention but then flows down to the bottom as consumption."
—Davade Thompson

"Quit taking chances and choose Christ."
—Davade Thompson

"You can never overdo what can be done better."
—Davade Thompson

"Did technology take away the knowledge of God?"
—Davade Thompson

"Be careful not to trust invention over Godly intervention."
—Davade Thompson

"It is never too late if God tells you to wait."
—Davade Thompson

"The best day of your life is when you choose to die in Christ."
—Davade Thompson

"You can never produce what you do not possess, but you can possess what you never produced."
—Davade Thompson

"With God being the head of your life, glory is always at the end of the story."
—Davade Thompson

"The most difficult enemy you will ever have to
fight is the one that you are in love with."
—Davade Thompson

"In order to stay saved, you must hide the word in your
heart and exclude the world from your thought."
—Davade Thompson

"Your thought is the road that leads to your heart."
—Davade Thompson

"Make it a habit to have blessings rehearsed and curses reversed."
—Davade Thompson

"Daily sorrows will build a sad tomorrow."
—Davade Thompson

"Success will always undergo trials because it is always
guilty of breaking the barriers of limitations."
—Davade Thompson

"Pleasure puts you in prison, but sacrifice makes you free."
—Tuxricko Lindsay

"Everybody is a novice (unskillful) at doing everything for the first time except pretending."
—Davade Thompson

"Evil should not be reciprocated but be laid to rest."
—Davade Thompson

"You will never fix your errors until you come
face to face with your past like a mirror."
—Camilla Dwyer

"Friends should be tested before they are trusted."
—Davade Thompson

"Winners proclaim, whiners complain."
—Davade Thompson

"Truth can be hidden in the dark, but lies are exposed in the light."
—Davade Thompson

"Make sure that anything you are a part of is always done in full."
—Davade Thompson

"There will never be another you, but there is always someone else who can do what you do. So be irreplaceable, irresistible, and unstoppable."
—Davade Thompson

"Success is like a magnifying glass, it makes small people look big."
—Tuxricko Lindsay

"Your degree has no power to declare nor decree."
—Davade Thompson

"Before you put on the whole armor, you
must first take off the old garment."
—Davade Thompson

"The timing is never perfect for the impatient."
—Davade Thompson

"In the multitude of friends success reveals an enemy."
—Tuxricko Lindsay

"There is nothing wrong with having guidelines,
but everything is wrong with having limits."
—Davade Thompson

"Not every wind you need to cease for some you need to sail."
—Davade Thompson

"It doesn't matter what you drive today, if you'll be walking tomorrow."
—Joseph X. Ledgister

"Having faith is more important than having sight. For
if you have faith, you can gain back your sight; if you
have sight, it can cause you to lose your faith."
—Davade Thompson

"You have to be willing to do what has never been done
before in order to prove what else is possible."
—Davade Thompson

"A wise man will observe when others are offended."
—Davade Thompson

"Transparency blocks out iniquity."
—Davade Thompson

"Dreams come for us to direct us to our purpose."
—Davade Thompson

"There is a thin line between love and hate, but there is none between unforgiveness and death, death and hell, and hell and the lake of fire."
—Davade Thompson

"Christianity is not insanity, it is only rejected reality."
—Davade Thompson

"Everyone can be normal, but not everyone can be loyal."
—Davade Thompson

"The difference between the ladder and the steps is that the ladder requires both hands and feet for climbing, while the steps only require your feet. But the similarity is that both takes you up. And so do not be discouraged if climbing takes more time and effort."
—Davade Thompson

"Your desire to be seen can cause you to be blind to others."
—Davade Thompson

"To fix our world, we must fix our countries; to fix our countries, we must fix our communities; to fix our communities, we must fix our people; and to fix our people, our people must fix their minds on God."
—Davade Thompson

"All of us will do better in the eyes of strangers but
will let lose once they become our friends."
—Davade Thompson

"It's good to knock doors but at some point
you must be the one who opens it."
—Davade Thompson

"Optionless will leave you faithful."
—Davade Thompson

"Organization will give you control of possession."
—Davade Thompson

"You have to embrace the future to erase the past."
—Davade Thompson

"Always have an open ear and not an itching one."
—Davade Thompson

"You will never be stretched by what is not beyond your reach."
—Davade Thompson

"Always make sure to bring something to the
table before you take away anything."
—Davade Thompson

"Developing your own way of doing things
is not selfish, it's just stylish."
—Davade Thompson

"Learn to seek God first and not after you have suffered the worst."
—Davade Thompson

"History repeats itself but you don't have to follow."
—Davade Thompson

"Knockers gain access, and seekers find secrets."
—Davade Thompson

"Strangers knock, but owners have keys."
—Davade Thompson

"Sometimes, people have to let you down before you believe in your own strength."
—Davade Thompson

"Upholding God's principle and his favor will forever add flavor to your life."
—Davade Thompson

"There is no liberty from slavery if your only desire is to trade time for money."
—Davade Thompson

"Be anxious for nothing, but be thankful for all."
—Davade Thompson

"Envy makes the carrier the enemy."
—Davade Thompson

"The catch to life is to try your best never to drop it."
—Davade Thompson

"The strength of any dream is measured by a contradicting reality."
—Davade Thompson

"What pushes me to work all night is when I think that if I don't I will then be in the same place tomorrow."
—Davade Thompson

"People will follow you if you show them that where you are going is worth coming."
—Davade Thompson

"Your imagination can build a nation."
—Davade Thompson

"Purpose is like a child waiting to become an adult. It can take a while before it happens; but once it comes, you can never get rid of it. If you do, failure will be your portion."
—Davade Thompson

"Every improvement starts with empowerment."
—Davade Thompson

"I stopped complaining about that which I don't have when I realized that even that which I have I don't deserve."
—Davade Thompson

"If you do not learn how to trust God then you could end up losing even that which you have."
—Davade Thompson

"Faith will be demonstrated in the area where hope is directed."
—Davade Thompson

"Success is yours when you learn how to make your difference a defense and not a deficiency."
—Davade Thompson

"The person that you are supposed to be with will love you because of what you hate about yourself."
—Davade Thompson

"It's better to have peace than war, but it will sometimes take a piece of you to have the peace you are looking for."
—Joseph X. Ledgister

"Be careful not to dream too long for it might just become a nightmare you cannot wake up from."
—Joseph X. Ledgister

"A crown of glory awaits the man who has Jesus as his head."
—Davade Thompson

"The love of money is the root of all evil, but the love of God roots up all evil."
—Davade Thompson

"Waste no time celebrating until you have crossed the finish line."
—Davade Thompson

"Desperation will always reign over mere desire."
—Davade Thompson

"Distance is no dispute if destiny is kept in view."
—Davade Thompson

"Familiarity breathes contentment, but disagreement brings contention."
—Davade Thompson

"The man who has influence is always seated higher than he who is on the throne."
—Davade Thompson

"Martin Luther King Jr. may not have made it to the White House, but his dream did."
—Davade Thompson

"Addiction is like trying to fill a well using a teaspoon."
—Davade Thompson

"Talent is never enough because success requires more."
—Davade Thompson

"Everyone that is engaged in the fight for salvation stands a chance of marrying freedom."
—Davade Thompson

"Study not only to memorize but also to understand, so that understanding will remind you if you lose your memory."
—Davade Thompson

"Truth stands alone but lies need companionship."
—Dr. Sidrell H. Williams

"Be careful of things that entice you to be excited in the wrong way."
—Dr. Sidrell H. Williams

"Temptation weakens you, but it doesn't cause you to fall."
—Sidrell H. Williams

"The strength to puruse and to prolong is in becoming the word."
—Sidrell H. Williams

"Your desire is a boiling pot that takes any ingredients."
—Sidrell H. Williams

"A man is not condemned because of what is in his closet, he is condemned because of what he chooses to wear."
—Davade Thompson

"Anybody can be saved, for even people that were once anti-Christ have become an adhesive for Christ."
—Sidrell H. Williams

"Lies hate truth but love weaknesses."
—Davade Thompson

"It takes discipline to stay committed and distraction to destroy purpose."
—Davade Thompson

"Never reject a stone for somebody might use it to hit you."
—Davade Thompson

"In order for you to know the power of resurrection, you must first die."
—Davade Thompson

"It doesn't matter who is speaking, no one motivates you more than someone whose fault is evident, but still they are confident about life."
—Davade Thompson

"Blindness carries no pride."
—Davade Thompson

"Integrity does not fight with atrocities."
—Sidrell H. Williams

"Christianity is never sweet until your motive is pure."
—Sidrell H. Williams

"Our service is never complete until the kingdom of God is added to by what we do."
—Sidrell H. Williams

"True repentance carries no residue."
—Davade Thompson

"A close mind will never see possibilities."
—Davade Thompson

"Worrying is more work than labor."
—Davade Thompson

"Better is the poor man that never became rich,
than the rich man that became poor."
—Sidrell Williams

"You can either learn by paying attention or by paying the price."
—Davade Thompson

"Willingness leaves no space for laziness."
—Davade Thompson

"The value of anything is determined by the need for it."
—Davade Thompson

"Insecurity is too risky because it leaves your
character without protection."
—Davade Thompson

"Honesty bares fruit of purity and truth."
—Davade Thompson

"A wise man does things while he has the drive for purpose and not when he loses the drive but still has the purpose."
—Sidrell Williams

"Quick deception brings you to quick failure."
—Sidrell Williams

"Subjection comes only when satisfaction is full."
—Sidrell Williams

"Pride will lift you up but not keep you up because it's intention is for you to fall."
—Davade Thompson

"If you have no option, it doesn't mean you will never have opposition."
—Davade Thompson

"Do everything worthwhile as if it is in high demand right now."
—Davade Thompson

"Every profession can answer man's desire, but only purpose can answer man's destiny."
—Davade Thompson

"Wisdom not only says the right thing, but it also finds the right person and says it at the right time."
—Davade Thompson

"Giving is not complete until receiving is fulfilled."
—Sidrell Williams

"Staying together is difficult if your interest lies somewhere else."
—Davade Thompson

"It is nice to look expensive but it is also expensive to look nice."
—Davade Thompson

"Racism is being against people for something they had no control over."
—Davade Thompson

"Life and death is in the power of the tongue, but the tongue has no power except that which the mind gives to it."
—Davade Thompson

"If the devil has eaten all he can from you and you still have leftovers, then it means that you are more than what the devil can manage."
—Davade Thompson

"It is hard being at peace if you are surviving on broken pieces; so let God mend you."
—Davade Thompson

"It is not over if you can start again."
—Davade Thompson

"If you complain, it doesn't stop the problem from happening again."
—Davade Thompson

"If by their fruits you shall know them, then fruit is the root of truth."
—Davade Thompson

"Do not use idols to replace the I AM."
—Davade Thompson

"Many times ignorance is our biggest hindrance to deliverance."
—Davade Thompson

"Fellowship is professional, friendship is personal."
—Joseph X. Ledgister

"Your next day is always predetermined by how you end your last night."
—JC

"Without faith, it is impossible to please God. And without God, it is impossible to please you."
—Davade Thompson

"There is no common person if they have an uncommon purpose."
—Davade Thompson

"In spite of our abilities, it is God who causes us to do things. For without God, our abilities are disabilities."
—Davade Thompson

"Ignoring the problem doesn't fix the crisis, but applying Christ does."
—Davade Thompson

"The winner's mentality says: run now, relax later."
—Davade Thompson

"Successful people have work time, rest time, but no free time. For time is too expensive for you to not make a profit from every single moment."
—Davade Thompson

"Fear is being faithful to a situation rather than to the solution."
—Davade Thompson

"A moment to think in silence can give you years that echoes the noise of success."
—Davade Thompson

"Working hard without being smart will be a punishment; working hard and being smart will bring you accomplishment."
—Davade Thompson

"As things and time change, you cannot change time but you can change things."
—Davade Thompson

"Sometimes, the things that make you look good are the things that make you lose God."
—Davade Thompson

"The empty soul doesn't seek for God unless its emptiness is accompanied by humility."
—Davade Thompson

"The companion of opinion is deception."
—Davade Thompson

"For the man whose gift did not make room, when it comes to purpose he will be left homeless."
—Davade Thompson

"Never let go of what you have in your hand unless there is something better to hold on to."
—Davade Thompson

"If the head is a clown, then the whole body becomes a circus."
—Davade Thompson

"If you are in a cycle, then your final stop will be your starting spot."
—Davade Thompson

"Jesus was a carpenter that led fishermen and so when they catch, he builds. Learn to make friends with different people that have similar purpose."
—Davade Thompson

"We can ignore the voice of constant warnings for as long as we want, but when life speaks we have no choice but to listen."
—Joseph Ledgister

"When our season comes the pain of past discipline, will becomes the strength of our character."
—Joseph Ledgister

"The sacrifices we make along the way, though painful, will bring us joy in the long run."
—Joseph Ledgister

"It's easy to live on the edge if you have nothing else to live for and if you are hanging on to success."
—Davade Thompson

"Forgiveness is a burden only to whom needs to be forgiven themselves."
—Sidrell Williams

"Faith cannot be held in the flesh, but in a diverse manifestation of the spirit."
—Sidrell Williams

"Silver and gold loses its value over time, but precious is the word that never grows old."
—Sidrell Williams

"Purposes are sustained through prayer, while habits are chastened desires."
—Sidrell Williams

"Love is not propagated in the ideas of people, but in people themselves."
—Sidrell Williams

"When the curtain of life falls, death becomes tragic because of its finalities."
—Sidrell Williams

"Many are seeking for happiness but rejects God who has it all."
—Davade Thompson

"Your desire should be to have vision and not attention."
—Davade Thompson

"Transformation may take place in your mind but it is revealed in your steps."
—Davade Thompson

"Your mistake oftentimes reveal God's mystery."
—Davade Thompson

"Man's conclusion is not God's limitation."
—Davade Thompson

"Do not conclude until you consider, do not confirm until you conclude."
—Davade Thompson

"Never complain until you comply."
—Dr. Sidrell H. Williams

"Money can only purchase what faith produced."
—Davade Thompson

"God recycles, repairs, and restores."
—Davade Thompson

"Trouble cannot endure because we've got a God that opens doors."
—Davade Thompson

"We can only get rid of haters by loving them because we become part of their family if we hate haters."
—Tuxricko Lindsay

"They said not even God can sink the titanic, well today it is still underwater a testimony to all generation to prove that God did do it."
—Davade Thompson

"Greatness is never at its greatest."
—Davade Thompson

"Purpose has got no weekend, so make everyday a workday."
—Davade Thompson

"Love knocks your door, but hate knocks it down."
—Davade Thompson

"Your secret is safer with the deaf than with the dumb, but yet the deaf would be the first one to speak it and not the dumb."
—Davade Thompson

"Success takes sacrifice, but failure could take you if you are satisfied."
—Davade Thompson

"Seek God early and he will never be late."
—Davade Thompson

"A man's gift will make room for him as soon as he lays the foundation."
—Davade Thompson

"Love build bridges, hate build boundaries, and unforgiveness build cages."
—Davade Thompson

"Productivity is an enemy to mediocrity but a friend to excellency."
—Davade Thompson

"You will always be lame if you find someone else to blame."
—Davade Thompson

"Don't just do what you love, love what you do and the results will change."
—Davade Thompson

"Push your performance if you want promotion."
—Davade Thompson

"Obstacles are ladders to see further."
—Davade Thompson

"The world makes duplicates, while the word makes disciples."
—Sidrell Willliams

"As high as the eagle sores, at some point it still has to eat off the ground. So humble yourself."
—Davade Thompson

"Affliction is for promotion."
—Davade Thompson

"The elephant wins versus the ant in size but loses to the ant through an open door."
—Davade Thompson

"You will never be satisfied with what you love."
—Davade Thompson

"Intimate is not immediate."
—Davade Thompson

"Anything that happens automatically takes faith."
—Davade Thompson

"Never fear being favored nor fair."
—Davade Thompson

"Your past will either be the reason why you can or an excuse why you cannot."
—Davade Thompson

"Change is not substitution, its progression."
—Camilla Dwyer

"It is impossible to truly know God's character and not serve him."
—Camilla Dwyer

"If tomorrow you will reign, then it doesn't matter if today it rains."
—Davade Thompson

"If there is no joy where you are going to, then there will be no strength in what you are going through."
—Davade Thompson

"Self-acceptance is opinion rejection."
—Davade Thompson

"You may not get what you sow, but you will certainly get what you grow."
—Davade Thompson

"Anyone that is carrying a cross is expected to be crucified."
—Davade Thompson

"Everything that is now an emergency you once had time to do."
—Davade Thompson

"Don't worry about people who started after you and past you by along the way because most of these are just construction without foundation."
—Davade Thompson

"Low self-esteem is like cancer to your character because it slowly eats away your confidence"
—Davade Thompson

"As rain becomes snow in the winter, so do fake friends become enemies in hard times."
—Davade Thompson

"You can either make problem a depression, or chose to press on."
—Davade Thompson

F-for
A-all
I-increase
T-trust
H-him
—Davade Thompson

W-way
I-I
L-live
L-life
—Davade Thompson

S-stand
T-through
I-it
L-little
L-longer
—Davade Thompson

"Having strong feet does not guarantee that you will stand after a defeat."
—Davade Thompson

"Many people are still breathing but are lifeless."
—Davade Thompson

"Your weakness is not something that you do not have the strength to do, but is something that you do not have the strength to stop doing."
—Davade Thompson

"Whatever the heart feels must be expressed in order to be understood because the heart can't be seen but a voice can be heard."
—Camilla Dwyer

"It's better to be a leader than a cheerleader."
Davade Thompson

"You can never love wicked people enough to stop them from hating you."
—Davade Thompson

About the Author

Camilla Dwyer always knew she wanted to be a writer, however she also knew that being born and raised in Jamaica meant that she would have to work twice as hard as her peers to achieve this goal. After migrating to Canada, Camilla perused a professional writing degree at York University in aims of accomplishing this dream and pursuing a future in writing. Camilla completed her degree 3 years ago and now mentians her writing through blogging as well as utilizing her professional writing skill in her everyday life.

Davade Thompson is a minister at the Holy Remnant Apostolic Church in Mississauga, Canada. He was born in Jamaica but migrated to Canada in his late teens with the desire of pursuing a career. However, God had a different plan. He quickly realized that all doors are locked to the desired pathway. He then sought counselling from different counsellors. But like many young people, he was left more confused than before. It was at this point that he was introduced to the ministry of Dr. Sidrell H. Williams who identified the gifts and the calling on his life. Today, Davade enjoys sharing the word of God and serving people. It is just amazing how fulling your life can be when you help to fill the lives of others.

CPSIA information can be obtained
at www.ICGtesting.com
Printed in the USA
LVOW03s0052230318
570889LV00002B/3/P